365 Best Inspiring Quotes to Elevate Your Life

Thea Stewart

Member of PageTitans

Please don't forget to follow me on Amazon:

https://amazon.com/author/theiastewart

This book may not be copied,
scanned, or distributed in any form,
whether electronic or printed,
without the prior written consent of
the author.

We would greatly appreciate it if
you could provide a review as we
love to receive feedback from our
customers. Thank you.

"Live your beliefs and you can turn the world around." Henry David Thoreau

"Be where you are; otherwise you will miss your life." Buddha

"Success is no accident. It is hard work, perseverance, learning, studying, sacrifice and most of all, love of what you are doing or learning to do." Pele

"Your victory is right around the corner. Never give up." Nicki Minaj

"We need to take risks. We need to go broke. We need to prove them wrong, simply by not giving up." Awkwafina

"You must find the place inside yourself where nothing is impossible." Deepak Chopra

"Stop being afraid of what can go wrong and start being positive about what can go right." Unknown

"Be happy for this moment. This moment is your life." Omar Khayyam

"Life imposes things on you that you can't control, but you still have the choice of how you're going to live through this." Celine Dion

"Curiosity about life in all of its aspects, I think, is still the secret of great creative people." Leo Burnett

"I'm not going to continue knocking that old door that doesn't open for me. I'm going to create my own door and walk through that." Ava DuVernay

"It is never too late to be wise." Daniel Defoe

"I don't believe in happy endings, but I do believe in happy travels, because ultimately, you die at a very young age, or you live long enough to watch your friends die. It's a mean thing, life." George Clooney

"All life is an experiment. The more experiments you make, the better." Ralph Waldo Emerson

"Learning how to be still, to really be still and let life happen—that stillness becomes a radiance." Morgan Freeman

"I'm going to be gone one day, and I have to accept that tomorrow isn't promised. Am I OK with how I'm living today? It's the only thing I can help. If I didn't have another one, what have I done with all my todays? Am I doing a good job." Hayley Williams

"If you want to live a happy life, tie it to a goal, not to people or things." Albert Einstein

"If my mind can conceive it, if my heart can believe it, then I can achieve it." Muhammad Ali

"Belief creates the actual fact."
William James

"You define your own life. Don't let other people write your script." Oprah Winfrey

"You have to be where you are to get where you need to go." Amy Poehler

"We can't retract the decisions we've made. We can only affect the decisions we're going to make from here." Nick Rice

"Find people who will make you better." Michelle Obama

"I've missed more than 9000 shots in my career I've lost almost 300 games. 26 times I've been trusted to take the game winning shot and missed. I've failed over and over and over again in my life. And that is why I succeed."
Michael Jordan

"I can't change the direction of the wind, but I can adjust my sails to always reach my destination."
Jimmy Dean

"When I was 17, I read a quote that went something like: 'If you live each day as if it was your last, someday you'll most certainly be right.' It made an impression on me, and since then, for the past 33 years, I have looked in the mirror every morning and asked myself: 'If today were the last day of my life, would I want to do what I am about to do today?' And whenever the answer has been." N." for too many days in a row, I know I need to change something." Steve Jobs

"Try to be a rainbow in someone's cloud." Maya Angelou

"Don't cry because it's over, smile because it happened." Dr. Seuss

"The more you praise and celebrate your life, the more there is in life to celebrate." Oprah Winfrey

"Don't allow your past or present condition to control you. It's just a process that you're going through to get you to the next level." T.D. Jakes

"Dig the Well Before You Are Thirsty." Chinese Proverb

"Tough times never last, but tough people do." Robert. H. Schuller

"I think if you live in a black-and-white world, you're gonna suffer a lot. I used to be like that. But I don't believe that anymore." Bradley Cooper

"Live for each second without hesitation." Elton John

"I enjoy life when things are happening. I don't care if it's good things or bad things. That means you're alive." Joan Rivers

"I have not failed, I have just found 10,000 ways that won't work." Thomas Edison

"Happiness is like a butterfly; the more you chase it, the more it will elude you, but if you turn your attention to other things, it will come and sit softly on your shoulder." Henry David Thoreau

"Hope is a good thing, maybe the best of things, and no good thing ever dies." Andy Dufresne, Shawshank Redemption

"Turn your wounds into wisdom." Oprah Winfrey

"Maybe that's what life is… a wink of the eye and winking stars." Jack Kerouac

"The two most important days in your life are the day you are born and the day you find out why." Mark Twain

"When you've seen beyond yourself, then you may find, peace of mind is waiting there." George Harrison

"The greatest pleasure of life is love." Euripides

"Failure happens all the time. It happens every day in practice. What makes you better is how you react to it." Mia Hamm

"Health is the greatest gift, contentment the greatest wealth, faithfulness the best relationship." Buddha

"Live as if you were to die tomorrow. Learn as if you were to live forever." Mahatma Gandhi

"If I cannot do great things, I can do small things in a great way."
Martin Luther King Jr.

"Life doesn't require that we be the best, only that we try our best."
H. Jackson Brown Jr.

"Today is a good day to try."
Quasimodo, The Hunchback of Notre Dame

"The purpose of life is not to be in control. It is to be connected."
Deepak Chopra

"Nothing is impossible. The word itself says: 'I'm possible!.'" Audrey Hepburn

"Being defeated is often a temporary condition. Giving up is what makes it permanent." Marilyn vos Savant

"Every master was once a disaster." T.S. Wood

"The simple act of listening to someone and making them feel as if they have truly been heard is a most treasured gift." L. A. Villafane

"It always seems impossible until it's done." Nelson Mandela

"It ain't about how hard you hit. It's about how hard you can get hit and keep moving forward." Sylvester Stallone in Rocky Balboa

"It is during our darkest moments that we must focus to see the light." Aristotle

"We all have problems. But it's not what happens to us, [it 's] the choices we make after." Elizabeth Smart

"You can be everything. You can be the infinite amount of things that people are." Kesha

"I like criticism. It makes you strong." LeBron James

"I want to be in the arena. I want to be brave with my life. And when we make the choice to dare greatly, we sign up to get our asses kicked. We can choose courage or we can choose comfort, but we can't have both. Not at the same time." Brene Brown

"You're not defined by your past; you're prepared by it. You're stronger, more experienced, and you have greater confidence." Joel Osteen

"In three words I can sum up everything I've learned about life: It goes on." Robert Frost

"There's more to life than basketball. The most important thing is your family and taking care of each other and loving each other no matter what." Stephen Curry

"Here's to the crazy ones. The misfits. The rebels. The troublemakers. The round pegs in the square holes. The ones who see things differently. They're not fond of rules. And they have no respect for the status quo. You can quote them, disagree with them, glorify or vilify them. About the only thing you can't do is ignore them. Because they change things. They push the human race forward. And while some may see them as the crazy ones, we see genius. Because the people who are crazy enough to think they can change the world, are the ones who do." Steve Jobs

"Life is about making an impact, not making an income." Kevin Kruse

"Never give up your desire to be what you want to be. Stay focused, persistent and relentless." Debasish Mridha MD

"If you spend your whole life waiting for the storm, you'll never enjoy the sunshine." Morris West

"In the long run, the sharpest weapon of all is a kind and gentle spirit." Anne Frank

"The purpose of life is not to be happy, but to matter, to be productive, to be useful, to have it make some difference that you lived at all." Leo Rosten

"When I was 5 years old, my mother always told me that happiness was the key to life. When I went to school, they asked me what I wanted to be when I grew up. I wrote down 'happy'. They told me I didn't understand the assignment, and I told them they didn't understand life." John Lennon

"If life were predictable it would cease to be life, and be without flavor." Eleanor Roosevelt

"Happy is the man who can make a living by his hobby." George Bernard Shaw

"Surround yourself with positive people." Rod Rohrich

"Failure is success in progress." Albert Einstein

"We all can dance when we find music that we love." Giles Andreae

"Anyway, like I was sayin', shrimp is the fruit of the sea. You can barbecue it, boil it, broil it, bake it, saute it. There's shrimp-kabobs, shrimp creole, shrimp gumbo. Pan fried, deep fried, stir-fried. There's pineapple shrimp, lemon shrimp, coconut shrimp, pepper shrimp, shrimp soup, shrimp stew, shrimp salad, shrimp and potatoes, shrimp burger, shrimp sandwich. That, that's about it." Bubba (Forrest Gump)

"Every strike brings me closer to the next home run." Babe Ruth

"Part of being a champ is acting like a champ. You have to learn how to win and not run away when you lose." Nancy Kerrigan

"You make a choice: continue living your life feeling muddled in this abyss of self-misunderstanding, or you find your identity independent of it. You draw your own box." Duchess Meghan

"Life is never easy. There is work to be done and obligations to be met obligations to truth, to justice, and to liberty." John F. Kennedy (JFK Quotes)

"Watch your thoughts; they become words. Watch your words; they become actions. Watch your actions; they become habits. Watch your habits; they become character. Watch your character; it becomes your destiny." Lao-Tze

"I have learned over the years that when one's mind is made up, this diminishes fear; knowing what must be done does away with fear." Rosa Parks

"Life isn't finding shelter in the storm. It's about learning to dance in the rain." Sherrilyn Kenyon

"When we strive to become better than we are, everything around us becomes better too." Paulo Coelho

"Stick around. Don't lose your heart, just keep going, keep at it." Mark Ruffalo

"Get busy living or get busy dying." Stephen King

"My mama always said, life is like a box of chocolates. You never know what you're gonna get." Forrest Gump (Forrest Gump Quotes)

"Identity is a prison you can never escape, but the way to redeem your past is not to run from it, but to try to understand it, and use it as a foundation to grow." Jay-Z

"I think I can. I think I can. I think I can. I know I can." Watty Piper, The Little Engine That Could

"The whole secret of a successful life is to find out what is one's destiny to do, and then do it." Henry Ford

"Winners never quit, and quitters never win." Vince Lombardi

"Whatever you think the world is withholding from you, you are withholding from the world." Eckhart Tolle

"Life is really simple, but we insist on making it complicated." Confucius

"Never bend your head. Always hold it high. Look the world straight in the eye." Helen Keller

"No matter what you're going through, there's a light at the end of the tunnel." Demi Lovato

"Everything negative pressure, challenges is all an opportunity for me to rise." Kobe Bryant

"It is our choices that show what we truly are, far more than our abilities." J. K. Rowling

"Let me tell you the secret that has led me to my goal. My strength lies solely in my tenacity." Louis Pasteur

"Every moment is a fresh beginning." T.S. Eliot

"Instead of letting your hardships and failures discourage or exhaust you, let them inspire you." Michelle Obama

"People tell you the world looks a certain way. Parents tell you how to think. Schools tell you how to think. TV. Religion. And then at a certain point, if you're lucky, you realize you can make up your own mind. Nobody sets the rules but you. You can design your own life." Carrie Ann Moss

"Never give up. Today is hard, tomorrow will be worse, but the day after tomorrow will be sunshine." Jack Ma

"Courage doesn't always roar, sometimes it's the quiet voice at the end of the day whispering 'I will try again tomorrow'." Mary Anne Radmacher

"The meaning of life is to find your gift. The purpose of life is to give it away." Pablo Picasso

"The longer I live, the more beautiful life becomes." Frank Lloyd Wright

"Football is like life, it requires perseverance, self-denial, hard work sacrifice, dedication and respect for authority." Vince Lombardi

"There are no regrets in life, just lessons." Jennifer Aniston

"We are not our best intentions. We are what we do." Amy Dickinson

"You only live once, but if you do it right, once is enough." Mae West

"Today, you have 100% of your life left." Tom Landry (Football Quotes)

"Don't settle for what life gives you; make life better and build something." Ashton Kutcher

"Work like there is someone working 24 hours a day to take it away from you." Mark Cuban

"Just don't give up trying to do what you really want to do. Where there is love and inspiration, I don't think you can go wrong." Ella Fitzgerald

"The power of imagination makes us infinite." John Muir

"There are three things you can do with your life: You can waste it, you can spend it, or you can invest it. The best use of your life is to invest it in something that will last longer than your time on Earth." Rick Warren

"Ambition is the path to success. Persistence is the vehicle you arrive in." Bill Bradley

"The man who moves a mountain begins by carrying away small stones." Confucius

"The only way to do great work is to love what you do." Steve Jobs

"Being the richest man in the cemetery doesn't matter to me. ... Going to bed at night saying we've done something wonderful ... that's what matters to me." Steve Jobs

"You must expect great things of yourself before you can do them." Michael Jordan

"Weaknesses are just strengths in the wrong environment." Marianne Cantwell

"There are no mistakes, only opportunities." Tina Fey

"Perfection is not attainable, but if we chase perfection we can catch excellence." Vince Lombardi

"The unexamined life is not worth living." Socrates

"I don't look ahead. I'm right here with you. It's a good way to be." Danny DeVito

"We have to be better. We have to love more, hate less. We've gotta listen more and talk less. We've gotta know that this is everybody's responsibility." Meghan Rapinoe

"I'm realizing how much I've diminished my own power. I'm not doing that no more." Alicia Keys

"There is nothing impossible to they who will try." Alexander the Great

"I'm as proud of many of the things we haven't done as the things we have done. Innovation is saying no to a thousand things."
Steve Jobs

"Life is very interesting… in the end, some of your greatest pains, become your greatest strengths."
Drew Barrymore

"Do not dwell in the past, do not dream of the future, concentrate the mind on the present moment."
Buddha

"I just want you to know that if you are out there and you are being really hard on yourself right now for something that has happened ... it's normal. That is what is going to happen to you in life. No one gets through unscathed. We are all going to have a few scratches on us. Please be kind to yourselves and stand up for yourself, please."
Taylor

"I know from experience that you should never give up on yourself or others, no matter what."
George Foreman

"You're braver than you believe, stronger than you seem, and smarter than you think." A. A. Milne

"A lot of people give up just before they're about to make it. You know you never know when that next obstacle is going to be the last one." Chuck Norris (related: 101 Chuck Norris Jokes)

"Don't be afraid to fail. It's not the end of the world, and in many ways, it's the first step toward learning something and getting better at it." Jon Hamm

"When you have a dream, you've got to grab it and never let go." Carol Burnett

"The greatest blessings of mankind are within us and within our reach. A wise man is content with his lot, whatever it may be, without wishing for what he has not." Seneca

"Sometimes you can't see yourself clearly until you see yourself through the eyes of others." Ellen DeGeneres

"Giving up is for rookies."
Philoctetes

"On one hand, we know that everything happens for a reason, and there are no mistakes or coincidences. On the other hand, we learn that we can never give up, knowing that with the right tools and energy, we can reverse any decree or karma. So, which is it? Let the Light decide, or never give up? The answer is: both." Yehuda Berg

"Your image isn't your character. Character is what you are as a person." Derek Jeter

"Not having the best situation, but seeing the best in your situation is the key to happiness." Marie Forleo

"Be courageous. Challenge orthodoxy. Stand up for what you believe in. When you are in your rocking chair talking to your grandchildren many years from now, be sure you have a good story to tell." Amal Clooney

"Work hard, know your s—t, show your s—t, and then feel entitled." Mindy Kaling

"You will meet two kinds of people in life: ones who build you up and ones who tear you down. But in the end, you'll thank them both." Anonymous

"When a defining moment comes along, you can do one of two things. Define the moment, or let the moment define you." Roy McAvoy

"Life is like riding a bicycle. To keep your balance, you must keep moving." Albert Einstein

"Life is not a problem to be solved, but a reality to be experienced." Soren Kierkegaard

"The moral of my story is the sun always comes out after the storm. Being optimistic and surrounding yourself with positive loving people is for me, living life on the sunny side of the street." Janice Dean

"If you live long enough, you'll make mistakes. But if you learn from them, you'll be a better person." Bill Clinton

"When we do the best we can, we never know what miracle is wrought in our life or the life of another." Helen Keller

"The greatest glory in living lies not in never falling, but in rising every time we fall." Nelson Mandela

"Being vulnerable is a strength, not a weakness." Selena Gomez

"It always seems impossible until it's done." Nelson Mandela

"Nobody who ever gave his best regretted it." George Halas

"It's not that I'm so smart, it's just that I stay with problems longer." Albert Einstein

"Success is not final, failure is not fatal: it is the courage to continue that counts." Winston Churchill

"Make each day your masterpiece." John Wooden

"With the right kind of coaching and determination you can accomplish anything." Reese Witherspoon

"It is impossible to live without failing at something, unless you live so cautiously, that you might as well not have lived at all in which case you fail by default." Anonymous

"Life is what happens when you're busy making other plans." John Lennon

"Clouds come floating into my life, no longer to carry rain or usher storm, but to add color to my sunset sky." Rabindranath Tagore

"If you don't like the road you're walking, start paving another one." Dolly Parton

"Life is a flower of which love is the honey." Victor Hugo

"Never let the fear of striking out keep you from playing the game." Babe Ruth

"Don't try to lessen yourself for the world; let the world catch up to you." Beyoncé

"I have learned to seek my happiness by limiting my desires, rather than in attempting to satisfy them." John Stuart Mill

"You must not lose faith in humanity. Humanity is an ocean; if a few drops of the ocean are dirty, the ocean does not become dirty." Mahatma Gandhi

"It's hard to beat a person who never gives up." Babe Ruth

"The best way to predict your future is to create it." Abraham Lincoln & Peter Drucker

"I refuse to quit because I haven't tried all possible ways yet." Unknown

"The only journey is the one within." Rainer Maria Rilke

"Life has got all those twists and turns. You've got to hold on tight and off you go." Nicole Kidman

"God helps those who persevere." The Koran

"The purpose of life is to be defeated by greater and greater things." Rainer Maria Rilke

"I am experienced enough to do this. I am knowledgeable enough to do this. I am prepared enough to do this. I am mature enough to do this. I am brave enough to do this." Alexandria Ocasio-Cortez in Knock Down The House

"The more man meditates upon good thoughts, the better will be his world and the world at large." Confucius

"Survival can be summed up in three words never give up. That's the heart of it really. Just keep trying." Bear Grylls

"You don't have to be defined or confined by your environment, by your family circumstances, and certainly not by your race or gender." Mariah Carey

"Silence is the last thing the world will ever hear from me." Marlee Matlin

"Be as you wish to seem." Socrates

"As we express our gratitude, we must never forget that the highest appreciation is not to utter words, but to live by them." John F. Kennedy

"Don't limit yourself. Many people limit themselves to what they think they can do. You can go as far as your mind lets you. What you believe, remember, you can achieve." Mary Kay Ash

"Not how long, but how well you have lived is the main thing." Seneca

"The secret of happiness, you see is not found in seeking more, but in developing the capacity to enjoy less." Socrates

"There may be people who have more talent than you, but there's no excuse for anyone to work harder than you do and I believe that." Derek Jeter

"The bad news is time flies. The good news is you're the pilot." Michael Altshuler

"The big lesson in life, baby, is never be scared of anyone or anything." Frank Sinatra

"Do all the good you can, for all the people you can, in all the ways you can, as long as you can." Hillary Clinton (inspired by John Wesley quote)

"Too many of us are not living our dreams because we are living our fears." Les Brown

"Don't give up. I believe in you all. A person's a person. No matter how small." Dr. Seuss

"You can't connect the dots looking forward; you can only connect them looking backward. So you have to trust that the dots will somehow connect in your future. You have to trust in something — your gut, destiny, life and karma, whatever. This approach has never let me down, and it has made all the difference in my life." Steve Jobs

"To conquer frustration, one must remain intensely focused on the outcome, not the obstacles." T.F. Hodge

"Wake up determined, go to bed satisfied." Dwayne." The Roc." Johnson

"Life is like a coin. You can spend it any way you wish, but you only spend it once." Lillian Dickson

"It had long since come to my attention that people of accomplishment rarely sat back and let things happen to them. They went out and happened to things." Leonardo Da Vinci

"How long should you try?
Until." Jim Rohn

"Live in the sunshine, swim the
sea, drink the wild air." Ralph
Waldo Emerson

"Many of the truths that we cling
to depend on our point of view."
Obi-Wan Kenobi (Star Wars)

"The minute that you're not
learning I believe you're dead."
Jack Nicholson

"Character consists of what you do on the third and fourth tries." James A. Michener

"How wild it was, to let it be." Cheryl Strayed

"When you feel like quitting think about why you started." Anonymous

"If you're going through hell, keep going." Winston Churchill

"If you run, you might lose. If you don't run, you're guaranteed to lose." Jesse Jackson

"Picasso had a saying. He said 'Good artists copy, great artists steal.' And we have always been shameless about stealing great ideas. ... I think part of what made the Macintosh great was that the people working on it were musicians and poets and artists and zoologists and historians who also happened to be the best computer scientists in the world." Steve Jobs

"Everything that's broken was beautiful at one time. And our mistakes make us better people." Jamie Hoang

"If you make your internal life a priority, then everything else you need on the outside will be given to you and it will be extremely clear what the next step is." Gabrielle Bernstein

"The way I see it, every life is a pile of good things and bad things. The good things don't always soften the bad things, but vice versa, the bad things don't always spoil the good things and make them unimportant." Doctor Who

"Out of difficulties grow miracles." Jean de la Bruyere

"Successful men and women keep moving. They make mistakes, but they don't quit." Conrad Hilton

"Keep smiling, because life is a beautiful thing and there's so much to smile about." Marilyn Monroe

"Take up one idea. Make that one idea your life -- think of it, dream of it, live on that idea. Let the brain, muscles, nerves, every part of your body be full of that idea, and just leave every other idea alone. This is the way to success." Swami Vivekananda

"Hold fast to your dreams, for without them life is a broken winged bird that cannot fly." Langston Hughes

"What lies behind you and what lies in front of you, pales in comparison to what lies inside of you." Ralph Waldo Emerson

"If you fall behind, run faster. Never give up, never surrender, and rise up against the odds." Jesse Jackson

"By perseverance the snail reached the ark." Charles Spurgeon

"The struggle you're in today is developing the strength you need for tomorrow. Don't give up." Robert Tew

"The way I see it, if you want the rainbow, you gotta put up with the rain." Dolly Parton

"You can't put a limit on anything. The more you dream, the farther you get." Michael Phelps

"It is when we are most lost that we sometimes find our truest friends." Brothers Grimm

"I've missed more than 9000 shots in my career. I've lost almost 300 games. 26 times I've been trusted to take the game winning shot and missed. I've failed over and over and over again in my life. And that is why I succeed." Michael Jordan

"It's never too late never too late to start over, never too late to be happy." Jane Fonda

"We have to let go of who we think we should be and embrace what is." Achea Redd

"You cannot control everything that happens to you; you can only control the way you respond to what happens. In your response is your power." Anonymous

"The purpose of life is not to be happy. It is to be useful, to be honorable, to be compassionate, to have it make some difference that you have lived and lived well." Ralph Waldo Emerson

"In every job that must be done, there is an element of fun. You find the fun and snap! the job's a game." Mary Poppins

"Dreams don't have to just be dreams. You can make it a reality; if you just keep pushing and keep trying, then eventually you'll reach your goal. And if that takes a few years, then that's great, but if it takes 10 or 20, then that's part of the process." Naomi Osaka

"In order for the light to shine so brightly, the darkness must be present." Sir Francis Bacon

"Life is what we make it, always has been, always will be." Grandma Moses

"I will not let anyone scare me out of my full potential." Nicki Minaj

"Life isn't about waiting for the storm to pass, it's about learning to dance in the rain." Vivian Greene

"You do not find the happy life. You make it." Camilla Eyring Kimball

"Either do not begin or, having begun, do not give up." Chinese Proverb

"The purpose of life is to discover your gift. The work of life is to develop it. The meaning of life is to give your gift away."
David Viscott

"To find something, anything, a great truth or a lost pair of glasses, you must first believe there will be some advantage in finding it." Jack Burden, All The King's Men

"When it comes to luck, you make your own." Bruce Springsteen

"That's been one of my mantras -- focus and simplicity. Simple can be harder than complex: You have to work hard to get your thinking clean to make it simple. But it's worth it in the end, because once you get there, you can move mountains." Steve Jobs

"Do you want to spend the rest of your life selling sugared water, or do you want a chance to change the world." Steve Jobs

"Good friends, good books, and a sleepy conscience: this is the ideal life." Mark Twain

"There should be no boundaries to human endeavor. We are all different. However bad life may seem, there is always something you can do, and succeed at. While there's life, there is hope." Stephen Hawking, The Theory of Everything

"You do what you can for as long as you can, and when you finally can't, you do the next best thing. You back up but you don't give up." Chuck Yeager

"Life is either a daring adventure or nothing at all." Helen Keller

"Happiness is the feeling that power increases that resistance is being overcome." Friedrich Nietzsche

"We should remember that just as a positive outlook on life can promote good health, so can everyday acts of kindness." Hillary Clinton

"When one door closes, another opens; but we often look so long and so regretfully upon the closed door that we do not see the one that has opened for us." Alexander Graham Bell

"We don't get a chance to do that many things, and every one should be really excellent. Because this is our life. Life is brief, and then you die, you know? And we've all chosen to do this with our lives. So it better be damn good. It better be worth it." Steve Jobs

"Just disconnect. Once in a day sometime, sit silently and from all connections disconnect yourself." Yoda (Star Wars Quotes)

"Life isn't about finding yourself. It's about creating yourself." George Bernard Shaw

"If you can do what you do best and be happy, you're further along in life than most people." Leonardo DiCaprio

"We become not a melting pot but a beautiful mosaic. Different people, different beliefs, different yearnings, different hopes, different dreams." Jimmy Carter

"When it is obvious that goals can't be reached, don't adjust the goals, but adjust the action steps." Confucius

"You are never too old to set another goal or to dream a new dream." C.S. Lewis

"There's nothing more powerful than not giving a f—k." Amy Schumer

"Don't be afraid. Because you're going to be afraid. But remember when you become afraid, just don't be afraid." Joan Jett

"What you get by achieving your goals is not as important as what you become by achieving your goals." Zig Ziglar

"Whether you think you can or think you can't you're right." Henry Ford

"Throughout life people will make you mad, disrespect you and treat you bad. Let God deal with the things they do, cause hate in your heart will consume you too." Will Smith

"It is our attitude at the beginning of a difficult task which, more than anything else, will affect its successful outcome." William James

"Many of life's failures are people who did not realize how close they were to success when they gave up." Thomas A. Edison

"Trying to grow up is hurting. You make mistakes. You try to learn from them, and when you don't, it hurts even more." Aretha Franklin

"At the end of the day, whether or not those people are comfortable with how you're living your life doesn't matter. What matters is whether you're comfortable with it." Dr. Phil

"If you love life, don't waste time, for time is what life is made up of." Bruce Lee

"The only limit to our realization of tomorrow will be our doubts today." Franklin Delano Roosevelt

"The purpose of human life is to serve and to show compassion and the will to help others." Albert Schweitzer

"I will love the light for it shows me the way, yet I will endure the darkness because it shows me the stars." Og Mandino

"Nothing is more honorable than a grateful heart." Seneca

"In order to write about life first you must live it." Ernest Hemingway

"Act as if what you do makes a difference. It does." William James

"As my knowledge of things grew I felt more and more the delight of the world I was in." Helen Keller

"Nurture your mind with great thoughts. To believe in the heroic makes heroes." Benjamin Disraeli

"You must do the things you think you cannot do." Eleanor Roosevelt

"It takes a dream to get started, desire to keep going, and determination to finish." Eddie Harris, Jr.

"Don't be discouraged. It's often the last key in the bunch that opens the lock." Unknown

"My Mama always said you've got to put the past behind you before you can move on." Forrest Gump

"Life would be tragic if it weren't funny." Stephen Hawking

"When you cease to dream you cease to live." Malcolm Forbes

"The healthiest response to life is joy." Deepak Chopra

"It's more fun to be a pirate than join the Navy." Steve Jobs

"Fall seven times, stand up eight." Japanese Proverb

"Never take life seriously. Nobody gets out alive anyway." Anonymous

"Life shrinks or expands in proportion to one's courage." Anais Nin

"If you have good thoughts they will shine out of your face like sunbeams and you will always look lovely." Roald Dahl

"I am the master of my fate: I am the captain of my soul." William Ernest Henley

"I care about decency and humanity and kindness. Kindness today is an act of rebellion." Pink

"Life is short, and it is here to be lived." Kate Winslet

"You just never give up. You do a task to the best of your abilities and beyond." Debbie Reynolds

"If we don't change, we don't grow. If we don't grow, we aren't really living." Gail Sheehy

"Nobody built like you, you design yourself." Jay-Z

"Life is a dream for the wise, a game for the fool, a comedy for the rich, a tragedy for the poor." Sholom Aleichem

"Ever tried. Ever failed. No matter. Try again. Fail again. Fail better." Samuel Beckett

"Living an experience, a particular fate, is accepting it fully." Albert Camus

"No one has the power to shatter your dreams unless you give it to them." Maeve Grayson

"I guess it comes down to a simple choice, really. Get busy living or get busy dying." Shawshank Redemption

"It takes 20 years to build a reputation and five minutes to ruin it. If you think about that, you'll do things differently." Warren Buffett

"I believe you make your day. You make your life. So much of it is all perception, and this is the form that I built for myself. I have to accept it and work within those compounds, and it's up to me." Brad Pitt

"For me, becoming isn't about arriving somewhere or achieving a certain aim. I see it instead as forward motion, a means of evolving, a way to reach continuously toward a better self. The journey doesn't end." Michelle Obama

"Real change, enduring change, happens one step at a time." Ruth Bader Ginsburg

"Definitions belong to the definers, not the defined." Toni Morrison

"You gain strength, courage, and confidence by every experience in which you really stop to look fear in the face. You are able to say to yourself, 'I lived through this horror. I can take the next thing that comes along.' You must do the thing you think you cannot do." Eleanor Roosevelt

"Success seems to be largely a matter of hanging on after others have let go." William Feather

"I believe that nothing in life is unimportant every moment can be a beginning." John McLeod

"I tell myself, 'You've been through so much, you've endured so much, time will allow me to heal, and soon this will be just another memory that made me the strong woman, athlete, and mother I am today'." Serena Williams

"My mission in life is not merely to survive, but to thrive; and to do so with some passion, some compassion, some humor, and some style." Maya Angelou

"Just because you fail once doesn't mean you're gonna fail at everything." Marilyn Monroe

"The best portion of a good man's life is his little nameless, unencumbered acts of kindness and of love." Wordsworth

"The purpose of our lives is to be happy." Dalai Lama

"No matter what people tell you, words and ideas can change the world." Robin Williams

"Find out who you are and be that person. That's what your soul was put on this earth to be. Find that truth, live that truth, and everything else will come." Ellen DeGeneres

"You choose the life you live. If you don't like it, it's on you to change it because no one else is going to do it for you." Kim Kiyosaki

"Keep your face always toward the sunshine, and shadows will fall behind you." Walt Whitman

"You have brains in your head. You have feet in your shoes. You can steer yourself any direction you choose." Dr. Seuss

"Don't give up, 'cos you have friends, don't give up, you're not beaten yet, don't give up, I know you can make it good." Peter Gabriel

"The next choice is the most important choice." George Wells

"It is never too late to be what you might have been." George Eliot

"Your time is limited, so don't waste it living someone else's life. Don't be trapped by dogma which is living with the results of other people's thinking." Steve Jobs

"Sing like no one's listening, love like you've never been hurt, dance like nobody's watching, and live like it's heaven on earth." Mark Twain

"Never give up on a dream just because of the time it will take to accomplish it. The time will pass anyway." Earl Nightingale

"Everybody wants to be famous, but nobody wants to do the work. I live by that. You grind hard so you can play hard. At the end of the day, you put all the work in, and eventually it'll pay off. It could be in a year, it could be in 30 years. Eventually, your hard work will pay off." Kevin Hart

"There is no failure except in no longer trying." Elbert Hubbard

"Out of the mountain of despair, a stone of hope." Martin Luther King, Jr.

"Never give up, for that is just the place and time that the tide will turn." Harriet Beecher Stowe

"As you know, life is an echo; we get what we give." David DeNotaris

"As you grow older, you will discover that you have two hands, one for helping yourself, the other for helping others." Audrey Hepburn

"Our lives are stories in which we write, direct and star in the leading role. Some chapters are happy while others bring lessons to learn, but we always have the power to be the heroes of our own adventures." Joelle Speranza

"We must let go of the life we have planned, so as to accept the one that is waiting for us." Joseph Campbell

"You don't always need a plan. Sometimes you just need to breathe, trust, let go and see what happens." Mandy Hale

"When we let fear be our master, we cannot be happy and free as a butterfly. But when we choose to trust the journey and embrace love and joy, we are free to fly."
Annicken R. Day

"You never really learn much from hearing yourself speak."
George Clooney

"I believe every human has a finite number of heartbeats. I don't intend to waste any of mine." Neil Armstrong

"Lieutenant Dan got me invested in some kind of fruit company [Apple computer]. So then I got a call from him, saying we don't have to worry about money no more. And I said, that's good! One less thing." Forrest Gump

"One day it started raining, and it didn't quit for four months. We been through every kind of rain there is. Little bitty stingin' rain... and big ol' fat rain. Rain that flew in sideways. And sometimes rain even seemed to come straight up from underneath. Shoot, it even rained at night..." Forrest Gump

"You're only human. You live once and life is wonderful, so eat the damned red velvet cupcake." Emma Stone

"Life is 10% what happens to us and 90% how we react to it." Charles R. Swindoll

"In the end, it's not the years in your life that count. It's the life in your years." Abraham Lincoln

"It does not matter how slowly you go as long as you do not stop." Confucius

"Remember to look up at the stars and not down at your feet. Try to make sense of what you see and wonder about what makes the Universe exist. Be curious. And however difficult life may seem, there is always something you can do and succeed at. It matters that you don't just give up." Stephen Hawking

"We've been making our own opportunities, and as you prove your worth and value to people, they can't put you in a box. You hustle it into happening, right." Jennifer Lopez

"If you're not stubborn, you'll give up on experiments too soon. And if you're not flexible, you'll pound your head against the wall and you won't see a different solution to a problem you're trying to solve." Jeff Bezos

"A lot of people are afraid to say what they want. That's why they don't get what they want." Madonna

"Life is a succession of lessons which must be lived to be understood." Helen Keller

"Once you figure out who you are and what you love about yourself, I think it all kinda falls into place." Jennifer Aniston

"The future rewards those who press on. I don't have time to feel sorry for myself. I don't have time to complain. I'm going to press on." Barack Obama

"Keep calm and carry on." Winston Churchill

"Embrace the glorious mess that you are." Elizabeth Gilbert

"It's really hard to design products by focus groups. A lot of times, people don't know what they want until you show it to them." Steve Jobs

"All you need is the plan, the road map, and the courage to press on to your destination." Earl Nightingale

"Do not allow people to dim your shine because they are blinded. Tell them to put some sunglasses on." Lady Gaga

"I've noticed when I fear something, if I just end up doing it, I'm grateful in the end." Colleen Hoover

"Your work is going to fill a large part of your life, and the only way to be truly satisfied is to do what you believe is great work. And the only way to do great work is to love what you do. If you haven't found it yet, keep looking. Don't settle. As with all matters of the heart, you'll know when you find it." Steve Jobs

"In a gentle way, you can shake the world." Mahatma Gandhi

"I believe that if you'll just stand up and go, life will open up for you. Something just motivates you to keep moving." Tina Turner

"You only pass through this life once, you don't come back for an encore." Elvis Presley

"Believe you can and you're halfway there." Theodore Roosevelt

"Life's tragedy is that we get old too soon and wise too late." Benjamin Franklin

"If opportunity doesn't knock, build a door." Milton Berle

"Just because someone stumbles and loses their path, doesn't mean they're lost forever." Professor X

"Happiness and influence and that which you seek to make your life complete." Louis Howard

"We generate fears while we sit. We overcome them by action." Dr. Henry Link

"Be nice to people on the way up, because you may meet them on the way down." Jimmy Durante

"Everyone has inside of him a piece of good news. The good news is that you don't know how great you can be! How much you can love! What you can accomplish! And what your potential is." Anne Frank

"Faith is love taking the form of aspiration." William Ellery Channing

"Money and success don't change people; they merely amplify what is already there." Will Smith